Becoming a Woman of excellence

NavPress is the publishing ministry of The Navigators, an international Christian organization and leader in personal spiritual development. NavPress is committed to helping people grow spiritually and enjoy lives of meaning and hope through personal and group resources that are biblically rooted, culturally relevant, and highly practical.

For a free catalog go to www.NavPress.com
or call 1.800.366.7788 in the United States or 1.800.839.4769 in Canada.

ISBN 978-1-57683-832-7

Cover design by Disciple Design
Cover photo by Getty Images
Creative Team: Dan Rich, Steve Parolini, Darla Hightower, Arvid Wallen, Glynese Northam

Some of the anecdotal illustrations in this book are true to life and are included with the permission of the persons involved. All other illustrations are composites of real situations, and any resemblance to people living or dead is coincidental.

Unless otherwise identified, all Scripture quotations in this publication are taken from the *New American Standard Bible* (NASB), © The Lockman Foundation 1960, 1962, 1963, 1968, 1971, 1972, 1973, 1975, 1977, 1995; Other versions used include: the *HOLY BIBLE: NEW INTERNATIONAL VERSION®* (NIV®), Copyright © 1973, 1978, 1984 by International Bible Society, used by permission of Zondervan Publishing House, all rights reserved; *The New Testament in Modern English* (PH), J. B. Phillips Translator, © J. B. Phillips 1958, 1960, 1972, used by permission of Macmillan Publishing Company; *The Living Bible* (TLB), Copyright © 1971, used by permission of Tyndale House Publishers, Inc., Wheaton, IL 60189, all rights reserved; the *Good News Bible Today's English Version* (TEV), copyright © American Bible Society 1966, 1971, 1976; the *Amplified Old Testament* (AMP), © 1962, 1964 by Zondervan Publishing, used by permission; the *Williams New Testament* (WMS) by Charles B. Williams, © 1937, 1965, 1966, by Edith S. Williams, Moody Bible Institute of Chicago; the *New Testament: An Expanded Translation* by Kenneth S. Wuest, © Wm. B. Eerdmanns Publishing Co. 1961. Used by permission; *The New English Bible* (NEB), © 1961, 1970, The Delegates of the Oxford University Press and The Syndics of the Cambridge University Press; the Holy Bible, *New Living Translation* (NLT), copyright © 1996. Used by permission of Tyndale House Publishers, Inc., Wheaton, Illinois 60189. All rights reserved; and the *King James Version* (KJV).

Heald, Cynthia
    Becoming a woman of excellence: a Bible study/by Cynthia Heald.
        114p. ; 22cm.
        Cover title: A Bible study on becoming a woman of excellence.
    ISBN 1-57683-832-3
        1. Women—Religious life. 2. Bible—Study and teaching. 3. Christian women—Conduct of life. 4. Success—Religious aspects. I. Bible study on becoming a woman of excellence.
    248.843 H434b

Printed in the United States of America

8 9 10 11 12 13 14 / 15 14 13 12 11

CYNTHIA HEALD

BECOMING A WOMAN OF *excellence*

NAVPRESS

Discipleship Inside Out™

The Quarry

His thoughts said, The time of preparation for service is longer than I had imagined it would be, and this kind of preparation is difficult to understand.

His Father said, "Think of the quarry whence came the stone for My house in Jerusalem."

The Tools

His thoughts said, I wonder why these special tools are used?

His Father said, "The house, when it was in building, was built of stone made ready before it was brought thither; so that there was neither hammer nor axe nor any tool of iron heard in the house, while it was in building.

"If thou knewest the disappointment it is to the builders when the stone cannot be used for the house, because it was not made ready before it was brought thither, if thou knewest My purpose for thee, thou wouldest welcome any tool if only it prepared thee quietly and perfectly to fit into thy place in the house."

—Amy Carmichael

My prayer is that this study will be a tool to prepare each of us to fit perfectly into His Kingdom.

—Cynthia Heald

CONTENTS

SUGGESTIONS FOR USING THIS STUDY

*B*ecoming a Woman of Excellence is suitable for group or individual study and for women of all ages, either married or single.

You'll notice personal reflections from the author in each chapter. Use these thoughts to prompt your examination and application of the study to your own life.

Most of the questions direct you into the Bible to help you formulate your answer based on the Word of God. Let the Scriptures speak to you personally; there is not always a right or wrong answer.

A verse for Scripture memory is given under the title of each chapter. You may memorize the verse before or after doing the chapter study, in any translation you choose.

A dictionary and any Bible references or commentaries can be good resources for you in answering questions. You'll also find them helpful in any further Bible study you might do on your own.

PREFACE

While reading through the book of Ruth, I was struck with Boaz's praise of Ruth: "Now my daughter, do not fear. I will do for you whatever you ask, for all my people in the city know that you are a woman of excellence" (Ruth 3:11).

My immediate response to this passage was to ask, What made Ruth a woman of excellence? As I studied her life, I discovered qualities within her that spoke strongly of strength and excellence. In prayer and further Bible study I learned that if we give priority attention to developing and maintaining ourselves inwardly as God desires, then our responses and actions will follow accordingly. Proverbs 4:23 says it well: "Watch over your heart with all diligence, for from it flow the springs of life." This study leads us into a discovery of how God's Word applies to our inner lives to challenge our commitment to excellence, to deepen our communion with God, and to prepare our hearts to proclaim the excellencies of Him who has called us out of darkness into His marvelous light (see 1 Peter 2:9).

As a result of my personal study, whenever I am confronted with choices or decisions of all kinds, I find myself asking the question, "What would a woman of excellence do?" May this be your question, too, as we become women of excellence for the honor and glory of God.

PART ONE

THE

GOAL

excellence

A GOAL WORTH PURSUING

*So that you may approve the things that are excel-
lent, in order to be sincere and blameless until the
day of Christ.*

PHILIPPIANS 1:10

*B*efore studying the book of Ruth, whenever I heard the word *excellence* associated with another person, I usually thought that they
were probably perfect, that they were high achievers, and that their lives
were generally good. So I was taken by surprise when I read Ruth's kins-
man, Boaz, respond to her by saying: "all my people in the city know
that you are a woman of excellence" (Ruth 3:11). I was surprised because
Ruth's life did not illustrate my understanding of excellence. Her husband
had died; she had left her own family, country, and future to move to a
foreign country and live with an unhappy mother-in-law. Her work was
foraging for leftover grain in a field. Yet, apparently, as she went about this
lowly task, those who knew her said, "Oh, Ruth, she has noble character,
she is strong, she is worthy."

In our world, beauty, ability in the marketplace, and independence
are major issues for women who search for meaning and excellence in

their lives. We are under pressure to choose the right clothes, the latest décor, and the most fashionable jewelry in order to establish our value as individuals. In our comparison shopping for material things, we often end up comparing ourselves with society's models of success and feel that no one would ever say to us, "I want to tell you that all my friends know you are a woman of excellence."

The Search for Excellence

1. What words or thoughts would you use to define *excellence*?

2. In today's world, how is excellence defined?

3. It is fairly easy to sense the world's view of excellence, but how would you describe or define the church's concept of excellence?

The church is in almost as much trouble as the culture, for the church has bought into the same value system: fame, success, materialism, and celebrity. We watch the leading churches and the leading Christians for our cues.[1]

Charles Colson

A Biblical View of Excellence

The Greek word translated "excellent" in the New Testament comes from *diapherō*, which literally means "transport" or "differ." In addition to "excellent," Scripture translations also use "best," "vital," "the better things," or "the highest and best."

The Hebrew word translated "excel" in Proverbs 31:29 is *'alah,* which means "to ascend."

Both these words are used to encourage us to ascend or transport or carry above the norm — to differ through the qualities of virtue and goodness.

Webster's dictionary defines *excel* as "to be superior or preeminent in good qualities or praiseworthy actions." *Excellence* is "the possession chiefly of good qualities in an unusual degree; surpassing virtue, merit, worth, value."

---

4. Three Scripture passages apply the concept of excellence to women. For each one, write down the qualities mentioned. (If your version doesn't use the actual term "excellent," write the equivalent phrase alongside your answer.)

   Ruth 3:11

Proverbs 12:4

Proverbs 31:10

The *Amplified Version* of the Bible seeks to give full meaning to key words in the original texts by suggesting a number of possible synonyms for a given word. Here is how this version renders the verses listed above:

Ruth 3:11—"a woman of strength—worth, bravery, capability"

Proverbs 12:4—"a virtuous and worthy wife—earnest and strong in character"

Proverbs 31:10—"a capable, intelligent and virtuous woman"

---

5. Look up the following verses to see what they teach about our pursuit of the "highest and best." For each reference, write down one specific thought that should affect how or why we strive for excellence.

1 Corinthians 10:31

Philippians 1:9-10

Philippians 4:8

6. If the goal of our pursuit is not clear, we risk losing sight of what it is we're striving for. The following Scripture passages give us specific guidelines for how we should pursue growth in our walk with God. What does each passage tell us to do?

Matthew 22:36-39

Romans 12:2

Colossians 1:9-10

2 Timothy 2:15

7. From the verses you've studied so far, how would you explain the biblical view of excellence to a friend?

A Personal Goal of Excellence

AUTHOR'S REFLECTION — As a young girl I remember my mother telling me many times, "If you are going to do anything, do it right!" This admonition was applied to setting the table, ironing a dress, or washing the dishes. My mom did not expect perfection, but her thought was that if I were to undertake a task, then I should do it to the best of my ability. I didn't realize it then, but early in my life I was being taught the value of doing things well.

When I reached my fortieth birthday, I realized that my life was probably half over! As I considered my past, I remembered my acceptance of Christ, college graduation, marriage, teaching English, several moves, and cooking, cleaning, and carpooling for four children. I felt that I was right where I needed to be, but somewhere over the years I had settled for a goal of mediocrity. I could identify with the secretary who had this sign over her desk: "Today I think I'll try to accomplish something . . . like getting through it!" At this stage in my life, I wanted to be sure that I was open to embrace all that God might have for me in my remaining years.

As I read through the Scriptures that year with this new perspective, I was able to see for the first time Boaz's comment to Ruth about her excellence. I immediately realized that she trusted God with her life and she did not allow her circumstances to dictate her behavior or responses. As I contemplated the qualities she had that made her a woman of noble character, I silently prayed, "Lord, I don't know how many years I have left to live, but I don't want to miss out on anything You have for me. For the rest of my life I want to be in the process of becoming a woman of excellence, a woman of noble character, for Your glory."

---

8. Take a few minutes and reflect on your life. Write down the ways you were encouraged to excel in life. Were these ways more help or hindrance to your understanding of excellence?

9. From each of these Scripture passages, select one important truth you need to grasp in order to have God's best for your life.

Philippians 3:12-14

Hebrews 6:1

Throughout our study we will be exploring not only God's call to excellence, but His provision, patience, and assurance that His power is perfected in weakness. From the beginning we need to realize that excellence is not perfection, but essentially a desire to be strong *in* the Lord and *for* the Lord. As Oswald Chambers wrote: "Do we so appreciate the marvellous salvation of Jesus Christ that we are our utmost for His highest?"[2]

10. Review any insights from this chapter that were especially meaningful to you in learning to become a woman of excellence. After thinking over the Scriptures you've studied, write down a goal you'd like to set for yourself in doing this study (for example, a possible goal might be, "To understand how I can become a woman of excellence"). Establishing a goal will help remind you of your purpose and commitment as you work through the study.

A Heart for God's Word

Scripture memory enables us to keep our goals in mind and open our hearts to the transforming work of the Holy Spirit. David wrote, "I delight to do Your will, O my God; Your Law is within my heart" (Psalm 40:8). Having God's Word in our hearts is great motivation to obey and to grow.

> I know of no other single practice in the Christian life more rewarding, practically speaking, than memorizing Scripture. That's right. No other single discipline is more useful and rewarding than this. No other single exercise pays greater spiritual dividends! Your prayer life will be strengthened. Your attitudes and outlook will begin to change. Your mind will become alert and observant. Your confidence and assurance will be enhanced. Your faith will be solidified.[3]
>
> *Charles R. Swindoll*

SUGGESTED SCRIPTURE MEMORY: Philippians 1:9-10

Notes

1. Charles Colson, *Loving God* (Grand Rapids: Zondervan, 1984), 14.

2. Oswald Chambers, *My Utmost for His Highest* (New York: Dodd, Mead & Co., 1966), July 7.

3. Charles R. Swindoll, *Growing Strong in the Seasons of Life* (Portland: Multnomah, 1983), 53.

excellence

GOD'S CHARACTER

*The LORD is my light and my salvation; Whom shall
I fear? The LORD is the defense of my life; Whom
shall I dread?*

PSALM 27:1

*I*f we are going to pursue a goal for our lives that reflects our desire
to understand and live up to the highest and best, then we need to
know God intimately—for He is our source and model of excellence.
Having a proper view of God is necessary if we are to live a life pleasing
to Him.

We must realize that a life with the goal of excellence cannot be lived
on our own merit or in our own strength. We know that we are not perfect, and that we will fail over and over again. How does God respond to
our imperfections and weaknesses?

First, we need to know and be reminded of God's unfailing and uncon-
ditional love, that His "power is perfected in weakness" (2 Corinthians
12:9) because of His tender and loving mercy toward us. Second, even
though God is the Creator and all-powerful, He cares about each of us
personally—and He has plans for us that will give us a future and a hope.

And third, we can trust our lives to a God who we know wants to meet our deepest needs, and desires only what is good for us.

As we study God's character, may we continue to be challenged to live a life reflecting His excellence.

> We must practice the art of long and loving meditation
> upon the majesty of God. This will take some effort, for
> the concept of majesty has all but disappeared from the
> human race.[1]
>
> *A. W. Tozer*

God's Loving Kindness

> How excellent is thy lovingkindness.
>
> *Psalm 36:7, KJV*

1. When asked to describe God's attributes, what comes to your mind?

2. Read the rich descriptions of God's character in the following passages. Which aspects of God's personhood are you most thankful for?

   Psalm 103:1-18

Psalm 145:8-21

---

3. Sometimes our view of God is determined by our relationship with our father or some other authority figure. If we have been brought up in a very strict, harsh home, for example, then we are likely to see God primarily as a judge. Truly believing that God is love is key to any response we have to Him.

Which characteristics of God, if any, do you find most difficult to accept because of your past experiences?

Pray over these characteristics that may be difficult for you to accept, and ask God to give you a fuller understanding of who He really is.

---

4. How would you describe the kind of love God has for us? Use Isaiah 49:15-16, Romans 5:8, 1 John 3:1, and other verses of your own choosing as the basis for your answer.

5. How does knowing that God loves you unconditionally and that you are His child affect your response to Him?

> Beloved, let us love. Lord, what is love? Love is that which inspired My life, and led Me to My Cross, and held Me on My cross. Love is that which will make it thy joy to lay down thy life for thy brethren. Lord, evermore give me this love. Blessed are they which do hunger and thirst after love, for they shall be filled.[2]
>
> *Amy Carmichael*

God's Sovereignty

> Praise Him according to His excellent greatness.
>
> *Psalm 150:2*

Sovereignty means *supreme power*. A. W. Tozer writes, "God's sovereignty is the attribute by which He rules His entire creation, and to be sovereign God must be all-knowing, all-powerful, and absolutely free . . . Free to do whatever He wills to do anywhere at anytime to carry out His eternal purpose in every single detail without interference."[3]

6. What do the following verses teach about God's sovereignty?

1 Chronicles 29:11-12

Psalm 115:3

Isaiah 46:9-10

Colossians 1:15-17

7. What do the following verses tell us about God's sovereign care for His people?

Jeremiah 29:11

John 16:33

Romans 8:28

What assurance and comfort do these verses give you as you encounter the trials and sorrows of life?

---

8. Whether we are Christians or not, there are trials to face in life. The difference in the Christian's life is that God's grace is sufficient to triumph through them and bear up under them. Study the following passages, and then write a paragraph giving a scriptural view of suffering. Psalm 119:71,75,76; John 9:1-3; 2 Corinthians 4:7-10; 2 Corinthians 12:7-10

No literature is more realistic and honest in facing the harsh facts of life than the Bible. At no time is there the faintest suggestion that the life of faith exempts us from difficulties. What it promises is preservation from all the evil in them. . . . All the water in all the oceans cannot sink a ship unless it gets inside. Nor can all the trouble in the world harm us unless it gets within us. That is the promise of [Psalm 121]: "The LORD will keep you from all evil."[4]

Eugene Peterson

---

9. Also essential to having some insight into hard times is recognizing the willfulness of our own sinful nature. Someone has said that God is a gentleman and He will not force His will on us; we must give Him permission to rule in our lives.

What do the following Scriptures teach about man's role in bringing trials on himself?

Psalm 81:8-14

Isaiah 48:17-19

Jeremiah 7:23-24

To believe actively that our Heavenly Father constantly spreads around us providential circumstances that work for our present good and our everlasting well-being brings to the soul veritable benediction. Most of us go through life praying a little, planning a little, jockeying for position, hoping but never being quite certain of anything, and always secretly afraid that we will miss the way. This is a tragic waste of truth and never gives rest to the heart.

There is a better way. It is to repudiate our own wisdom and take instead the infinite wisdom of God. Our insistence upon seeing ahead is natural enough, but it is a real hindrance to our spiritual progress. God has charged Himself with full responsibility for our eternal happiness and stands ready to take over the management of our lives the moment we turn in faith to Him.[5]

A.W. Tozer

---

10. What other examples from Scripture or your own life show a relationship between our actions and God's allowing our choices to affect the circumstances of our lives?

God's Provision

Praise the LORD in song, for He has done excellent things.

Isaiah 12:5

11. Read Psalm 23.

a. David used his own experience of being a shepherd to write the beautiful twenty-third psalm. How does a shepherd care for and provide for his sheep?

b. Since the Lord is our Shepherd, how does God provide for us?

c. What does this provision mean to you personally?

When the Lord is my Shepherd he is able to supply my needs, and he is certainly willing to do so, for his heart is full of love, and there *"I shall not want."* I shall not lack for *temporal things.* Does he not feed the ravens, and cause the lilies to grow? How, then, can he leave his children to starve? I shall not want *for spirituals,* I know that his grace will be sufficient for me. Resting in him he will say to me, "As thy day, so shall thy strength be."[6]

C. H. Spurgeon

12. What do the following verses teach about who meets our needs for security and protection?

Psalm 27:1

Psalm 91:4,14-16

Romans 8:31-32

2 Peter 1:3-4

Be assured, if you walk with Him and look to Him and expect help from Him, He will never fail you. As an older brother who has known the Lord for forty-four years, who writes this, says to you for your encouragement that He has never failed him. In the greatest difficulties, in the heaviest trials, in the deepest poverty and necessities, He has never failed me; but because *I was enabled by His grace to trust Him* He has always appeared for my help. I delight in speaking well of His name.[7]

George Mueller

AUTHOR'S REFLECTION—Early in my life I responded to God's love for me. Knowing that God loves me unconditionally has freed me from trying to live the Christian life by being perfect and trying to earn His love by performing. My understanding of God's constancy in His love encourages me to return His love by living a life which would bring honor to Him. I want to become a woman of excellence not because I have to perform, but because I choose to please God.

Because of my security and worth in Jesus Christ, I do not have to look to people or things to feel of value or loved. I am now free to love and serve because I can trust my needs to be met by my heavenly Father.

Your Response

13. Is there a new thought about God that has challenged or encouraged you? How can it make a difference in your life?

SUGGESTED SCRIPTURE MEMORY: Psalm 27:1. (You might want to write it on a 3" x 5" card, put it over the sink or wherever you will see it regularly, and memorize it. Thank God for who He is and for what He is doing in your life.)

Resources

C. S. Lewis. *The Problem of Pain.* New York: Macmillan, 1943.

Warren & Ruth Myers. *Experiencing God's Attributes* (a Bible study workbook). Colorado Springs: NavPress, 1984.

J. B. Phillips. *Your God Is Too Small.* New York: Macmillan, 1961.

Edith Schaeffer. *Affliction.* Old Tappan, N.J.: Fleming H. Revell, 1979.

A.W. Tozer. *The Knowledge of the Holy.* San Francisco: Harper & Row, 1961.

Notes

1. A. W. Tozer, *The Knowledge of the Holy* (San Francisco: Harper & Row, 1961).

2. Amy Carmichael, *If* (Grand Rapids: Zondervan, 1972).

3. Tozer, 115.

4. Eugene Peterson, *A Long Obedience in the Same Direction* (Downers Grove: InterVarsity, 1980), 38.

5. Tozer, 69.

6. Charles Haddon Spurgeon, *The Treasury of David,* Vol. One: Psalm I to LVII (McLean, Virginia: MacDonald Publishing Co., n.d.), 354.

7. George Mueller, in *Streams in the Desert,* compiled by Mrs. Charles E. Cowman (Minneapolis: World Wide Publications, 1979), 19-20.

CHAPTER THREE

excellence

BECOMING LIKE CHRIST

I press on toward the goal for the prize of the upward call of God in Christ Jesus.
PHILIPPIANS 3:14

*B*ecause God loves us to the extent that He is committed to our future welfare and to meeting our deepest needs, He desires for us to grow—to become like Christ. Our desire to excel and be strong delights Him, but we must allow Him to teach us that excellence is a life-long process and that *He* is our only source of strength. Growth occurs when we maintain our walk with God—remembering that the Christian life is a *process,* rather than giving up in frustration because we just can't live up to perfect standards. To *become* means to come into existence, to come to be, to undergo change or development. As we respond to His desire to be totally involved in our lives, we begin to change and to become like Christ.

There is a great market for religious experience in our world; there is little enthusiasm for the patient acquisition of virtue, little inclination to sign up for a long

33

apprenticeship in what earlier generations of Christians called holiness.[1]

Eugene Peterson

God's Desire for Us

1. In each of the following passages, what does God communicate about His relationship to us?

Psalm 149:4

Jeremiah 29:13

Matthew 11:28-30

Ephesians 2:4-7

Are there insights in these verses that especially encourage you to seek God's presence and work in your life? If so, what are they?

2. A biblical definition of becoming could be called *sanctification.* To "sanctify" means to make holy: sanctification is *growing* in divine grace as a result of Christian commitment.

What critical truths do the following verses teach about the process of becoming like Christ?

Romans 8:28-29

1 Corinthians 1:4-9

Philippians 1:6

Philippians 2:13

(*Special note*: In order to pattern our lives after Jesus, we need to first enter into a relationship with Him so that we can live in His strength—not our own. If you do not know Jesus as your personal Savior and Lord, would you consider the verses and booklets mentioned at the end of this chapter?)

In order to avoid discouragement and reliance on ourselves, it is important to know that God has begun His work in us, and He will complete it. But how encouraging to realize also that God is patient with the process! Oswald Chambers has challenged us, "Think of the enormous leisure of

God! He is never in a hurry." Moses was in the desert forty years before he led the Israelites out of Egypt. Joseph was in prison approximately nine years before Pharaoh called him out to interpret a dream and put him in charge of the Egyptian kingdom. Paul was in Tarsus several years before going on his first missionary journey.

---

3. What do these Scripture passages reveal about God's perspective of time?

    2 Peter 3:8-9

    Habakkuk 2:1-3

---

4. How do the Scriptures you have studied so far in this chapter encourage your perspective concerning your own personal growth in the Lord?

---

5. In Philippians 3:12-14, Paul explains his key to the process of becoming. What is it? How does Paul's response to God's process encourage your life?

AUTHOR'S REFLECTION—God desires to have fellowship with us, He is committed to our growth, and He is realistic in understanding where we are in our relationship to Him. So often we are the ones who put high expectations on ourselves as we try to live the Christian life in our own strength. When we trust in ourselves, we are destined to fail and then tempted to give up the whole idea of living a life that would be pleasing to God.

One example in my life has been my efforts to control my tongue. It has taken years of reading the Bible, praying, and memorizing Scripture before I have seen any progress in controlling my tongue. Growing in any area of the Christian life takes time, and the key is daily sitting at the feet of Jesus. Grasping the truths Jesus shares in John 15 has enabled me to experience some measure of victory in my life. I'm not perfect, but I am in the process of becoming. As a wise old saint once said, "I ain't what I ought to be, but I ain't what I used to be either!"

---

6. Read John 15:1-11 carefully before answering the following questions.

What are the key words in this passage?

What does it mean to abide or remain?

Why is it necessary to abide?

What are the benefits of abiding?

What are the results of not abiding?

What is one way of knowing that we are abiding?

Abiding has been defined as "the continual act of laying aside everything that I might derive from my own wisdom and merit, in order to draw all of this from Christ."

> It needs time to grow into Jesus the Vine: do not expect to abide in Him unless you will give Him that time . . . . Come, my brethren, and let us day by day set ourselves at His feet, and meditate on this word of His, with an eye fixed on Him alone. Let us set ourselves in quiet trust before Him, waiting to hear His holy voice — the still small voice that is mightier than the storm that rends the rocks — breathing its quickening spirit within us, as He speaks: "Abide in Me."[2]
>
> *Andrew Murray*

7. What do you think are some practical ways to answer the question, "How do I abide in Jesus?" (John 8:31 may be a helpful reference here.)

> The Scriptures were given not to increase our knowledge, but to change our lives.
>
> *D. L. Moody*

Our Desire for God

> Prayer — secret, fervent, believing prayer — lies at the root of all personal godliness.
>
> *William Carey*

8. Read and reflect on the following Scriptures. Write down the imagery that is used to describe desire for God.

Psalm 42:1-2

Psalm 63:1

Psalm 84:1-2

Why do you think the psalmists felt so strongly in their desire for God?

---

9. *Meditation* might be defined as prayerful reflection on the Word of God with a goal of application and understanding.

What are the benefits of meditation revealed in Psalm 1:1-3?

What are some possible ways you can meditate on God's Word day and night?

---

10. Looking back over this chapter, take some time to evaluate your desire for God. What draws you to abide in Christ? What hinders your spending time with Him?

11. If you would like, take a few minutes to come up with some creative
language (poetic imagery or a word picture) that helps capture how you
feel about drawing close to God. Put your words in the form of a prayer
to God.

SUGGESTED SCRIPTURE MEMORY: Philippians 3:14

> There is only one relationship that matters, and that is
> your personal relationship to a personal redeemer and
> Lord. Let everything else go, but maintain that at all costs,
> and God will fulfill His purpose through your life.[3]
> *Oswald Chambers*

If you do not have a personal relationship with Jesus Christ, prayerfully
consider the following verses, and speak to a friend or pastor who could
help you in understanding your relationship to Christ.

Romans 3:23
Romans 6:23
John 14:6
John 11:25-27
Romans 10:9-13

These booklets can help you in relating to and growing in Christ:
Steps to Peace with God (Billy Graham Evangelistic Association)
The Bridge Illustration (NavPress)
Seven Minutes with God (NavPress)
The Quiet Time (InterVarsity)
Lessons on Assurance (NavPress)

Notes

1. Eugene Peterson, *A Long Obedience in the Same Direction*, 12.

2. Andrew Murray, *Abide in Christ* (Springdale, Penn.: Whitaker House, 1980), 7, 15.

3. Oswald Chambers, *My Utmost for His Highest*, November 30.

PART TWO

THE

COST

excellence

ROOTED IN SURRENDER

*I have been crucified with Christ, and I myself no
longer live, but Christ is living in me; the life I now
live as a mortal man I live by faith in the Son of
God who loved me and gave Himself for me.*

GALATIANS 2:20, WMS

*T*he more time we spend with God praying and meditating on
His Word, the more we find our focus in life changing from self-
centeredness to Christ-centeredness. John the Baptist summed up the
process of becoming by proclaiming, "He must grow greater and greater,
but I less and less." Fenelon expresses the same thought: "Whatever spiritual knowledge or feelings we may have, they are all a delusion if they do
not lead us to the real and constant practice of dying to self."[1] To die to
self, or to surrender, means to give up, relinquish, yield, let go, abandon,
submit, give up my rights.

As we seek to become like Christ and to learn to abide in the Vine,
however, we begin to encounter some opposition. Tozer writes, "It would
seem that there is within each of us an enemy which we tolerate at our
peril. Jesus called it 'life' and 'self,' or as we would say, the self-life. To

allow this enemy to live is in the end to lose everything. To repudiate it and give up all for Christ's sake is to lose nothing at last, but to preserve everything unto life eternal."[2]

"I Myself No Longer Live . . . "

> There is only one thing God wants in us, and that is unconditional surrender.[3]
>
> *Oswald Chambers*

1. In John 12:24-25, Jesus sets forth some conditions and results related to our surrender before God. What are they?

2. Richard Foster defines self-denial as "simply a way of coming to understand that we do not have to have our own way."[4] In Luke 9:23 Jesus outlines a three-point program for discipleship. Write a brief explanation of each point.

When Jesus mentioned self-denial and cross-bearing, what did he really mean? (Mark 8:34). Many think of self-denial as giving up something during the Lenten season. Others have said that it is to be dead to self, or even to hate self. I disagree with these opinions. When Jesus referred to self-denial, he was not talking about denying ourselves some luxury item or denying the reality of self or the needs of self. Rather, he was focusing on the importance of renouncing self as the center of our life and actions. In other words, self-denial is the decision of each of his followers to give over to God his body, career, money, and time. A true disciple is willing to shift the spiritual center of gravity in his life. Self-denial is the sustained willingness to say no to oneself in order to say yes to God. . . . The cross . . . is the symbol of mission, essence of purpose . . . Whatever mission God gives me is my cross.[5]

Bill Hull

---

3. In his letter to the Philippians, Paul writes of his own personal surrender. Read Philippians 3:1-11. How does his example of yielding his life challenge you? (In answering this question, it might help you to note what Paul surrendered as well as his purpose for giving it up.)

You have trusted Him as your dying Savior; now trust Him as your living Savior. Just as much as He came to deliver you from future punishment did He also come

to deliver you from present bondage. Just as truly as He
came to bear your stripes for you has He come to live
your life for you.[6]

Hannah Whitall Smith

AUTHOR'S REFLECTION—When my husband Jack and I moved to a new
town some years ago, we had three small children all under three years
old. Jack was beginning his veterinary practice. Because he treated large
and small animals, he was usually gone 12-14 hours a day. Besides having
three small children, an absent husband and father, we lived in a very old
house that had mice! I had no close friends—only One, who heard my
cry, "Lord! I can't go on anymore. I'm tired, I'm lonely, I want to give up."
Unmistakably, I heard God's voice in my heart saying, "Good. I don't want
you to go on in your own strength. I want to live your life for you." That
was my initial surrendering. From that time on I began to understand
that the Christian life is not *imitation*, but *habitation*. It's an exchanged
life—His life for my life. Really, it's not an even exchange, as Elisabeth
Elliot says: "What is ours belongs to Christ, but also what is His belongs
to us!" Since I'm still in the process of becoming, I am continually challenged to surrender circumstances to Him daily. When I'm irritable and
frustrated over situations I cannot control, God will gently ask, "Cynthia,
whose life is it?" I have to answer, "It's yours, Lord, it's yours."

"But Christ Is Living in Me"

4. Read Colossians 3:1-4 and Galatians 2:20. How do these verses help you
   in your understanding of what it means to surrender?

> The Spirit of God witnesses to the simple almighty security of the life hid with Christ in God.[7]
>
> *Oswald Chambers*

---

5. Meditate on Paul's prayer in Ephesians 3:16-19. Personalize this prayer by using "I," "me," and "my" for the word "you," and write it out in the space below. Use this as your prayer often to renew your awareness of Christ's living in you.

6. In 1982, Lydia Joel was head of the Performing Arts dance department in New York City. *Parade Magazine* quoted part of her lecture to freshman dancers.

> This is an absolutely undemocratic situation you face. You have no rights here. Your only right is to come to class and be wonderful. You can't protest, you can't be absent, you can only work. . . . You must give your entire self in an act of faith. If you have any sort of resentment or lack of clarity, you will find heartbreak. But if you manage to live through four years of this demand upon your inner self, your life will be literally changed.[8]

a. What were these students asked to give up?

b. What was their motivation for surrendering?

c. What was their reward?

d. What does God ask of you?

e. What should be your motivation?

f. What are the rewards and benefits of your yielding?

g. Why is the process of giving up so often a struggle? (Paul's discussion in Romans 7:14-25 of his own struggle may yield some helpful insights here.)

In C. S. Lewis' book *The Screwtape Letters*, Screwtape (Satan) writes letters of instruction to his demon nephew, Wormwood, on how to keep a Christian from growing. Here he explains to Wormwood the doctrine of surrender (through this dialogue, Lewis highlights a key result of God's grace in our lives): "When He talks of their losing their selves, He means only abandoning the clamour of self-will; once they have done that, He really gives them back all their personality, and boasts (I am afraid, sincerely) that when they are wholly His they will be more themselves than ever."[9]

7. In Romans 8:12-14, Paul sums up his discussion of living by the Spirit versus living according to our sinful nature. What does he tell us to do?

8. It's been said, "It's not how much we have of the Holy Spirit that matters, but how much the Holy Spirit has of us." The key is always submitting and abandoning ourselves to God. "We have to keep letting go, and slowly and surely the great full life of God will invade us in every part, and men will take knowledge of us that we have been with Jesus."[10]

Has there been a time in your life when you have voluntarily handed your life over to God?

If yes, describe your experience.

If no, would you prayerfully consider surrendering your life now? Here is a suggested prayer from Hannah Whitall Smith:

> Here, Lord, I abandon myself to thee. I have tried in every way I could think of to manage myself, and to make myself what I know I ought to be, but have always failed. Now I give it up to thee. Do thou take entire possession of me. Work in me all the good pleasure of thy will. Mold and fashion me into such a vessel as seemeth good to thee. I leave myself in thy hands, and I believe thou wilt, according to thy promise, make me into a vessel unto thy own honor, "sanctified, and meet for the master's use, and prepared unto every good work."[11]

SUGGESTED SCRIPTURE MEMORY — Galatians 2:20. As you hide this verse in your heart, and as you live day by day, ask God to bring to mind your commitment to surrender *all* of your life to Him.

> George Mueller's secret:
> "There was a day when I died:
> • Died to George Mueller: to his tastes, his opinions, his preferences and his will.
> • Died to the world — its approval or censure.
> • Died to the approval or blame even of my brethren and friends.
> Since then I have studied only to show myself approved unto God."

Notes

1. Fenelon, *Let Go* (Springdale, Penn.: Whitaker House, 1973), 6.

2. A. W. Tozer, *The Pursuit of God* (Harrisburg, Penn.: Christian Publications, Inc., n.d.), 23.

3. Oswald Chambers, *My Utmost for His Highest*, October 23.

4. Richard Foster, *Celebration of Discipline* (San Francisco: Harper & Row, 1978), 99.

5. Bill Hull, *Jesus Christ, Disciplemaker* (Colorado Springs: NavPress, 1984), 170.

6. Hannah Whitall Smith, *The Christian's Secret of a Happy Life* (Westwood, N.J.: Fleming H. Revell, n.d.), 53.

7. Chambers, December 24.

8. Lydia Joel, as quoted in *Parade Magazine*, August 22, 1982.

9. C. S. Lewis, *The Screwtape Letters* (Old Tappan, N.J.: Fleming H. Revell, 1979), 59.

10. Chambers, April 12.

11. Whitall Smith, 39.

excellence

EXEMPLIFIED BY OBEDIENCE

For it is God who works in you to will and to act according to his good purpose.
PHILIPPIANS 2:13, NIV

The life hid with God is a hidden life, as to its source, but it must not be hidden as to its practical results. People must see that we walk as Christ walked, if we say that we are abiding in Him. We must prove that we 'possess' that which we 'profess.'"[1] A one-word summary of Hannah Whitall Smith's thoughts could be *obedience*. Obedience is submission, habitually yielding to authority. If we have surrendered our lives to God, then it will be natural to want to yield to His authority, to obey His commands and to please Him by living His way.

But obedience is not forced; it is motivated by a heart of love. David wrote in Psalm 40:8, "I desire to do your will, O my God; your law is within my heart" (NIV). John Flavell commented, "Your delight and readiness in the paths of obedience is the very measure of your sanctification."[2] Why has God asked us to obey Him, and how do we habitually submit?

Obeying for Our Good

1. Deuteronomy 10:12-13 summarizes some key aspects of the Christian life. As you read these verses, write down what we are asked to do and why we should keep or obey the Lord's commandments.

Oh that they had such a heart in them, that they would
fear Me and keep all My commandments always, that it
may be well with them and with their sons forever!

Deuteronomy 5:29

2. Psalm 119 expresses a wholehearted love for God's Word. What does each of the following verses tell you about the psalmist's attitudes toward God's commands?

verse 2

verse 129

verse 167

3. Often I will be prompted by the Holy Spirit to call a friend, write a letter, or serve someone in a special way. I will respond by thinking, *Yes, that's a good idea, I'll do that,* but then there are times I never get around to following through. Jesus taught about this particular attitude toward obedience. Read Matthew 21:28-32 and Luke 6:46-49 and write a brief paragraph summarizing His teaching on obedience. What is the major lesson in it for you?

In C. S. Lewis' *The Screwtape Letters,* Screwtape (Satan) instructs his demon nephew, Wormwood, on how to keep his Christian "patient" from obeying the Lord. Here is part of his letter: "Let him do anything but act. No amount of piety in his imagination and afflictions will harm us if we can keep it out of his will."[3]

How very true that is! The Greek word *hypakouō* is translated "to obey." It means to listen to, to answer. Jesus taught that a wise man hears and acts. How we listen to God and His Word determines our response.

4. Read Genesis 2:8–3:7. This passage relates the first command given (Genesis 2:16-17) and the first disobedience (Genesis 3:6-7). After reading these verses carefully, record your thoughts about the questions below.

   a. Explain Satan's temptation of Eve and why you think Eve responded as she did.

b. Do you think it's possible that Eve felt God's command was not really for her good—because it *denied* her something, rather than promising to protect her? Why might she have felt this way?

c. Note the similarities between Eve's progression to disobedience (Genesis 3:6) and the progression in James 1:13-15. What can you learn about yielding to temptation from these verses?

d. Paul wrote, "And it was not Adam who was deceived, but the woman being deceived, fell into transgression" (1 Timothy 2:14). To deceive means to cause to accept what is false, especially by trickery or misrepresentation.[4] Why do you think Eve was so easily deceived? What could Eve have done to avoid Satan's deception?

e. From your study of Eve, which thoughts challenge you in your own obedience to God?

---

5. Lot's wife had also been given a specific command before the destruction of Sodom. Read Genesis 19:15-17 and 19:26. Why do you think she looked back?

What can you learn from her example about obedience and God's purpose in giving us commands?

Obeying with His Power

> Our Lord never insists upon obedience; He tells us very emphatically what we ought to do, but He never takes means to make us do it. We have to obey Him out of a oneness of spirit.[5]
>
> *Oswald Chambers*

6. It is our choice to obey or disobey God. His desire is voluntary submission. If we desire to yield to Him in what He has asked us to do, then we are not alone in our goal of obedience. How do these Scriptures encourage us in our obedience?

   Isaiah 30:21

   Philippians 2:13

   Philippians 4:13

Amy Carmichael writes, "Do I *will* to do the will of God? Then God will reinforce my will and enable me to *do*. Do I *will* to know the will of God? Then I will not take into consideration my own feelings and interest, 'for even Christ pleased not Himself'—'never once consulted His own pleasure'"[6] (Romans 15:3).

---

7. Read Matthew 4:1-11 and note how Jesus countered Satan's temptations.

Examine the chart below that parallels the temptation of Eve and the temptation of Jesus. Write down what you learn about Satan's tactics and what you can do to strengthen the part of your life in which you feel most vulnerable.

Temptation	Genesis 3	Matthew 4
Appeal to physical appetite	You may eat of any tree (3:1)	You may eat by changing stones to bread (4:3)
Appeal to personal gain	You will not die (3:4)	You will not hurt your foot (4:6)
Appeal to power or glory	You will be like God (3:5)	You will have all the world's kingdoms (4:8-9)

The *Wuest* translation of 1 John 2:16-17 says: "Because everything which is in the world, the passionate desire of the flesh, and the passionate desire of the eyes, and the insolent and empty assurance which trusts in the things that serve the creature life, is not from the Father as a source but is from the world as a source. And the world is being caused to pass away, and its passionate desires. But the one who keeps on habitually doing the will of God abides forever."

AUTHOR'S REFLECTION — For me, obedience issues are related not so much to temptations to yield to evil as they are to struggles to do what I should. Procrastination, over-commitment to activities, and not living my priorities are my battlefields in this area. James wrote, "Therefore, to one who knows the right thing to do and does not do it, to him it is sin" (4:17). Most of my temptations and testings involve a choice to engage in activities that, although basically good in themselves, might come at the expense of my walk with God, my family, or other responsibilities. Just as Eve was deceived into thinking that she would become wise by eating the fruit, so I am often misled into wrong choices because I think they are good.

Joshua at one time entered into a covenant of peace with the Gibeonites, although God had clearly instructed that they were to be conquered. Joshua and the elders were deceived by circumstances, and it is recorded in Joshua 9:14 that they "did not ask for the counsel of the LORD."

If only Eve had sought the counsel of God. If only I would take time to ask God's thoughts concerning my decisions. James wrote that if we lack wisdom when encountering trials and testings in our lives, we should ask God for direction. *The Living Bible* paraphrases James 1:5, "If you want to know what God wants you to do, ask him, and he will gladly tell you, for he is always ready to give a bountiful supply of wisdom to all who ask him; he will not resent it." If I want to become a woman of excellence, I will take time to ask, listen, and then act.

Obeying for Our Growth

Above anything else, God's desire for us is that we become like His Son. We find in Scripture that Jesus "learned obedience from the things which He suffered" (Hebrews 5:8). Certainly one of the major ways that God has for us to learn obedience and to grow strong in our faith is by resisting temptations and persevering through trials. Jesus is our model; just as He was tempted and tried, so must we be challenged in the same way. How we respond to various testings reveals whether or not we have a heart to obey.

8. Paul tells us to have the same attitude as Christ. What attitude did Jesus manifest in order to become obedient? (Philippians 2:5-8)

9. Read James 1:2-4 and 1 Peter 1:6-7. What are the purposes of trials, and how should we respond to them?

It is important to note that James did *not* say that a believer should be joyous *for* the trials, but *in* the trials. . . . Stress deepens and strengthens a Christian's faith and lets its reality be displayed.[7]

---

10. What is promised to those who learn obedience through suffering?

James 1:12

James 5:11

1 Peter 5:10

"It was good for me to be afflicted so that I might learn your decrees" (Psalm 119:71, NIV).

"The present circumstance, which presses so hard against you, (if surrendered to Christ) is the best shaped tool in the Father's hand to chisel you for eternity. Trust Him, then. Do not push away the instrument lest you lose its work."[8]

We could define obedience as *willingly submitting to the process God has chosen for us to be conformed to the image of His Son.*

---

11. Is there a situation in your life with which you are struggling? How can you begin to specifically respond in a biblical way to this trial?

---

12. As you look back over your study in this chapter, can you see any specific ways in which the Lord might be leading you to strengthen your obedience to Him?

SUGGESTED SCRIPTURE MEMORY — Philippians 2:13

> The very best proof of your love for your Lord is obedience
> ... nothing more, nothing less, nothing else.
>
> *Charles R. Swindoll*

Jesus has said: "And you are my friends if you obey me" (John 15:14, TLB).

Notes

1. Hannah Whitall Smith, *The Christian's Secret of a Happy Life*, 250.

2. John Flavell, as quoted in *The Treasury of David*, by C. H. Spurgeon, 248.

3. C. S. Lewis, *The Screwtape Letters*.

4. *Roget's Thesaurus in Dictionary Form*, ed. Norman Lewis, s.v. "deceive."

5. Oswald Chambers, *My Utmost for His Highest*, November 2.

6. Amy Carmichael, *Thou Givest . . . They Gather* (Ft. Washington, Penn.: Christian Literature Crusade with Dohnavur Fellowship, 1958), 114.

7. *The Bible Knowledge Commentary*, ed. John F. Walvoord & Roy B. Zuck (Wheaton: Victor Books, 1983), 27.

8. Mrs. Charles E. Cowman, *Streams in the Desert*, 214.

PART THREE

THE

PRIZE

excellence

Molded by Discipline

Apply your heart to discipline and your ears to words of knowledge.
PROVERBS 23:12

Jesus Christ is the perfect example of the disciplined person. When the need of the hour was to fast, He was able to fast; when feasting was appropriate, He was free to feast. When teaching was needed, He always had the life-giving message; when silence was appropriate, He had the power to "speak not a word."

"In contrast to the rigidity of the Scribes and Pharisees, Jesus was always responsive to the word of the Father. He was able to disregard 'the traditions of men' when the appropriate response was to obey 'the word of God.' When a perfect sacrifice was needed for our redemption, Jesus was free to despise the shame and become 'obedient unto death on a cross.' When we see Jesus, we understand that discipline is liberating, life-giving, jubilant."[1]

The Necessity of Discipline

1. Proverbs 25:28 tells us, "A person without self-control is as defenseless as a city with broken-down walls." How does lack of self-control leave you defenseless?

   a. Proverbs 23:13 tells us to apply your heart to discipline. When you think of discipline, what comes to your mind?

   b. How does the dictionary define discipline? (Proverbs 25:28)

2. A good outline for 2 Peter 1:2-8 could be power, promises, and practice. Read these verses carefully. What is God's part and what is our part in our growth in faith? (See also 2 Timothy 1:7 and Galatians 5:22-23.)

Add to your faith virtue . . . (2 Peter 1:5). "Add" means there is something we have to do. We are in danger of forgetting that we cannot do what God does, and that God will not do what we can do. We cannot save ourselves nor sanctify ourselves, God does that; but God will not give us good habits, He will not give us character, He will not make us walk aright. We have to do all that ourselves, we have to work out the salvation God has worked in. "Add" means to get into the habit of doing things.[2]

Oswald Chambers

3. Below are verses that use different Greek words for discipline.[3] Look up the verses and write the English equivalent found in your Bible translation in the column below.

References	Greek	English Equivalent
Titus 2:5 Romans 12:3 2 Timothy 1:7	*sōphrōn* (to be of sound mind)	
Galatians 5:23 2 Peter 1:6	*enkrateia* (power over oneself)	
1 Timothy 4:7 Hebrews 5:14	*gymnazō* (train)	

We would do well to think of the Christian life as the path of disciplined Grace. It is discipline, because there is work for us to do. It is Grace, because the life of God which we enter into is a gift which we can never earn. Lovingly God works his life into us by Grace alone, joyfully we hammer out the reality of this new life on the anvil of discipline. Remember, discipline in and of itself does not make us righteous; it merely places us before God. Having done this, discipline has reached the end of its tether. The transformation . . . is God's work.[4]

Richard Foster

Areas of Discipline: Our Mind

4. In Romans 12:2 (NLT) we read, "let God transform you into a new person by changing the way you think." God has given us specific instructions concerning our minds. What are we asked to do in the following verses?

Isaiah 26:3

2 Corinthians 10:5

Colossians 3:2

Why do you think such emphasis is placed on the mind?

---

5. Read Romans 8:6-8. What do these verses say about the mind?

> This passage [Romans 8:6-8] makes it abundantly
> clear that the way one thinks is intimately related to
> the way one lives, whether in Christ, in the Spirit and
> by faith, or alternatively in the flesh, in sin and in spiri-
> tual death.[5]

Our Will

> It is sometimes thought that the emotions are the governing power in our nature. But I think all of us know, as a matter of practical experience, that there is something within us, behind our emotions and behind our wishes, an independent self, that, after all, decides everything and controls everything. Our emotions belong to us, and are suffered and enjoyed by us, but they are not ourselves; and if God is to take possession of us, it must be into this central will or personality that He enters.[6]
>
> *Hannah Whitall Smith*

6. Our response to God should never be contingent upon how we *feel*. From the following passages, write down the instances you find in which the psalmist exercised his will.

   Psalm 101:1-4

   Psalm 119:101,173

Our Emotions

Christian psychologist Larry Crabb teaches that right thinking and right behavior lead to right feelings.[7] Our emotions are consequences of our thinking and actions. So it is important that we discipline our minds and wills. When we have been hurt or rejected, though, our emotions can overpower us and we can feel helpless. I have found it helpful to immediately acknowledge exactly how I feel to God. After I have let Him know my feelings, I am usually able to exercise my will and choose to think the truth. Often the truth I need to remind myself of is that God loves me and is for me and that He will guide me in doing what is needed and what is right.

---

7. One of the best ways of handling our emotions is to fully acknowledge our feelings to God. Read Psalm 109. David was angry, hurt, and felt rejected. Write down any observations you can make about David's expression of emotion to God.

What conclusions resulted after David's time with God (verses 30-31)?

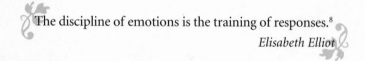

The discipline of emotions is the training of responses.[8]

Elisabeth Elliot

---

8. In Lamentations, Jeremiah acknowledges his feelings to God also. Read through Lamentations 3:1-26.

   a. What were Jeremiah's feelings before verse 21?

   b. What was Jeremiah's *thinking* after verse 21?

(Note the importance of not dwelling on our feelings but of exercising our wills to think the truth.)

> Cease to consider your emotions, for they are only the servants; and regard simply your will, which is the real king in your being. Is that given up to God? Does your will decide to believe? Does your will choose to obey? . . . And when you have got hold of this secret . . . that you need not attend to your emotions but simply to the state of your will, all the Scripture commands to yield yourself to God, to present yourself a living sacrifice to Him, to abide in Christ, to walk in the light, to die to self, become possible to you; for you are conscious that in all these your will can act, and can take God's side; whereas, if it had been your emotions that must do it, you would, knowing them to be utterly uncontrollable, sink down in helpless despair.[9]
>
> *Hannah Whitall Smith*

Our Bodies

9. Scripture reminds us that our bodies are the temple of the Holy Spirit (1 Corinthians 6:19). What instructions (or examples) are given in Romans 12:1 and in 1 Corinthians 9:24-27 concerning our bodies?

Why do you think it is important to honor and discipline our bodies?

> She girds herself with strength (spiritual, mental and
> physical fitness for her God-given task) and makes her
> arms strong and firm.
>
> *Proverbs 31:17*, AMP

Our Time

10. There are numerous seminars and books to tell us how to manage our
    time. Usually, it's not more information that we need, just more disci-
    pline! Someone has said, "There is always enough time to do the will of
    God." Would you agree with that statement? Why or why not?

11. What is the purpose of making the most of our time?

    Ephesians 5:15-17

    Psalm 90:12

One of Satan's most useful tools is getting us to waste time or to procras-
tinate. C. S. Lewis' Screwtape again writes Wormwood concerning his
patient's use of time: "All the healthy and outgoing activities which we
want him to avoid can be inhibited and *nothing* given in return, so that at

last he may say, as one of my own patients said on his arrival down here, 'I now see that I spent most of my life in doing *neither* what I ought *nor* what I liked.'"[10]

AUTHOR'S REFLECTION — Certainly excellence in our lives is molded by discipline. Jesus' words are so true: "Keep watching and praying that you may not come into temptation; the spirit is willing, but the flesh is weak" (Mark 14:38). So often my intentions are good, but I never follow through because I don't exercise my will over my feelings or my lazy body! Richard Foster said, "The disciplined person is the person who can do what needs to be done when it needs to be done."[11]

Two cautions concerning discipline: First *discipline is not rigid.* It does not mean that my schedule can never be interrupted. Foster writes: "The disciplined person is a flexible person. . . . The disciplined person is always free to respond to every movement of divine Grace."[12] When I am disciplined I am usually caught up with my responsibilities and can handle a change of plans and interruptions. It is when I'm behind and undisciplined that I find it hard to be flexible. The second caution is, *discipline should never become legalistic.* Swindoll has defined legalism as "conformity to a standard for the purpose of exalting self." The purpose of our discipline should be to order our lives in such a way that we are available to be used by God.

---

12. After studying the different facets of our lives that often need self-control, which area of your life do you feel needs more discipline? Why?

What could you begin to do now to develop self-control in that area?

A man may be consecrated, dedicated, and devoted, but of little value if undisciplined.

Hudson Taylor

13. Perhaps you would like to make a short-term goal for each area we have studied. Use this chart if you find it helpful.

Area	Goal	(Possible goals)
Mind		Consistent Scripture memory Reading plan for the Bible or other Christian books
Will		Something you need to say "No" or "Yes" to? Decide to cooperate with God in choosing to do what is right.
Emotions		Keep a journal expressing your feelings to God.
Body		Consistent exercise Balanced diet
Time		Make a priority list each day and at least try to get the most important item accomplished!

SUGGESTED SCRIPTURE MEMORY: Proverbs 23:12

I think this meditation by Joseph Bayly expresses my feelings toward discipline. I don't want to have regrets at the end of the day because I have been totally undisciplined. I want my focus to be on the Lord and pleasing Him.

> Lord Christ
> Your Servant
> Martin Luther
> said he only had
> two days
> on his calendar:
> today
> and "that day."
> And that's
> what I want too.
> And I want
> to live
> today
> for
> *that day.*

Notes

1. Richard Foster, "And We Can Live By It: Discipline," in *Decision Magazine,* September 1982, 11.

2. Oswald Chambers, *My Utmost for His Highest,* May 10.

3. The Greek is taken from *The New International Dictionary of New Testament Theology,* Vol. 3, ed. Colin Brown (Grand Rapids: Zondervan, 1971), 502, 494, 496, 313.

4. Foster, 11.

5. *Dictionary of New Testament Theology,* 617.

6. Hannah Whitall Smith, *The Christian's Secret of a Happy Life*, 80.

7. Larry Crabb, in a seminar at Glen Eyrie, Colorado Springs, January 1984.

8. Elisabeth Elliot, *Discipline: The Glad Surrender* (Old Tappan, N.J.: Fleming H. Revell, 1982), 15.

9. Whitall Smith, 84-85.

10. C. S. Lewis, *The Screwtape Letters*.

11. Foster, 10.

12. Foster, 10.

CHAPTER SEVEN

excellence

GUARDED BY DISCRETION

Discretion will guard you, understanding will watch over you, to deliver you from the way of evil.

PROVERBS 2:11-12

Solomon wrote, "As a ring of gold in a swine's snout so is a beautiful woman who lacks discretion" (Proverbs 11:22). Our looks, abilities, and knowledge fade into the background if discretion is not evident in our behavior. Learning to exercise discretion is essential to becoming a woman of excellence, for a woman who wants to please God by her life will honor him with gracious and thoughtful speech and actions.

Discretion has been defined as saying and doing the right thing in the right way at the right time. Bill Gothard defines discretion as the ability to avoid words, actions, and attitudes that could result in undesirable consequences. Discretion comes from the Greek word, *sōphrōn*, meaning sound mind, self-controlled, sane, temperate, sensible.[1] Applying discretion in our everyday lives will help us so that we will never be misplaced jewelry!

Discretion Defined

1. For a well-rounded understanding of discretion, look up the following words in the dictionary. Jot down the primary and secondary meanings.

    discreet—

    discretion—

    prudence—

    self-controlled—

    sensible—

2. Proverbs is a major scriptural source for learning about wisdom, knowledge, understanding, and discretion. What observations about discretion can you make from the following verses?

    Proverbs 2:11

Proverbs 5:1-2

Proverbs 8:12

---

3. Read Titus 2:3-5. Why do you think Paul asked the older women to teach discretion, or self-control, to the younger women?

Discretion Demonstrated:
Slow to Speak

4. How do these Proverbs describe one who is discreet or indiscreet in her conversation?

Proverbs 15:28

Proverbs 17:27-28

Proverbs 18:13

Proverbs 29:20

Remember this, my dear brothers! Everyone must be quick to listen, but slow to speak and slow to become angry. Man's anger does not achieve God's righteous purpose.

James 1:19-20, TEV

---

5. Esther was a Jewish woman who was chosen to be the queen of Persia. During her reign, the king's prime minister, Haman, convinced the king to sign an edict to destroy all the Jews in the land. Mordecai, Esther's cousin, encouraged her to approach the king about the edict to slaughter the Jews.

Read Esther 4:15–7:10.

What do you think helped Esther to be able to wait in sharing what was on her heart? (Had I been in her position, I would have immediately exposed the evil Haman and emotionally appealed to my husband's conscience!)

How does Esther exemplify discretion?

---

6. Read Luke 2:15-20. After all that Mary, the mother of Jesus, had witnessed of God's miraculous work in her life, how did she respond?

How do you think Mary exemplified discretion?

---

7. What guidelines does Paul provide in Ephesians 4:29 for those who want to be discreet?

If I can enjoy a joke at the expense of another; if I can in any way slight another in conversation, or even in thought, then I know nothing of Calvary love.[2]

Amy Carmichael

Slow to Anger

8. "A [woman's] discretion makes [her] slow to anger, and it is [her] glory to overlook a transgression" (Proverbs 19:11). What do these Proverbs have to say about being slow to anger?

Proverbs 12:16

Proverbs 15:1

Proverbs 16:32

The key to patience under provocation is to seek to develop God's own trait of being "slow to anger": (Exodus 34:6). . . . The best way to develop this slowness to anger is to reflect frequently on the patience of God toward us. The parable of the unmerciful servant (Matthew 18:21-35) is designed to help us recognize our own need of patience toward others by recognizing the patience of God toward us. . . . We are like the unmerciful servant when we lose our patience under provocation. We ignore God's extreme patience with us. We discipline our children out of anger, while God disciplines us out of love. We are eager to punish the person who provokes us, while God is eager to forgive. We are eager to exercise our authority, while God is eager to exercise his love. This kind of patience does not ignore the provocations of others; it simply seeks to respond to them in a godly manner.[3]

Jerry Bridges

Dresses Discreetly

9. What guidelines are given in 1 Timothy 2:9-10 to "women making a claim to godliness" in regard to their dress?

Do these verses apply to us today? If so, how?

10. In 1 Peter 3:3-4, what perspective does Peter add to our consideration of how we dress?

Plans Ahead

11. Part of prudence is the ability to have foresight. What do the following verses teach about "planning ahead"?

   Proverbs 14:15

   Proverbs 31:21

   Proverbs 31:25,27

12. Matthew 25:1-13 records the parable of the ten virgins. What does Jesus teach us about foresight in this story?

AUTHOR'S REFLECTION — Discretion is such a need in my life that I have memorized Psalm 69:5-6: "O God, it is You who knows my folly, and my wrongs are not hidden from You. May those who wait for You not be ashamed through me, O Lord GOD of hosts; may those who seek You not be dishonored through me, O God of Israel." These verses are special because I don't want my lack of discretion to be an embarrassment or hindrance to others.

To apply discretion in my life, I have set these goals:

- *slow to speak — trying to remember to think before I speak.*
- *slow to anger — being slow to anger not only toward my family, but toward those whom I don't know who frustrate me! (Other drivers, people who wait or don't wait on me in stores, etc.)*
- *dressing discreetly — trying not to attract or detract attention by the way I dress.*
- *planning ahead — making a basic schedule and keeping a list of things that need to be done in the future.*

Our purpose for being discreet is given in Titus 2:5 — "that the word of God will not be dishonored."

Discretion Applied

13. To guard means to defend, to keep in safety, to provide or secure against objections or attacks. After studying discretion, how do you think discretion can guard your life?

14. Applying discretion to our lives brings immediate results. Being slow to speak or slow to anger will become quickly evident to those close to us!

    What needs do you have in the area of discretion?

What is one specific thing you can begin to do to meet that need? (For example: memorize a verse, become accountable to an older woman in the Lord, ask someone's opinion of your dress, get a notebook and begin to plan ahead.)

SUGGESTED SCRIPTURE MEMORY: James 1:19

The LORD give you discretion and understanding.

1 Chronicles 22:12

Notes

1. *The Analytical Greek Lexicon Revised*, ed. Harold K. Moulton (Grand Rapids: Zondervan, 1978), 396.

2. Amy Carmichael, *If*.

3. Jerry Bridges, *The Practice of Godliness* (Colorado Springs: NavPress, 1983), 207-208.

excellence

MADE PRECIOUS BY A GENTLE AND QUIET SPIRIT

Your beauty should not be dependent on an elaborate coiffure, or on the wearing of jewellery or fine clothes, but on the inner personality — the unfading loveliness of a calm and gentle spirit, a thing very precious in the eyes of God.

1 PETER 3:3-4, PH

A woman with a gentle and quiet spirit is not only precious to God, but she is attractive to others also. Certainly a hallmark quality of a woman of excellence is a gentle and quiet spirit. A woman with this quality is not someone who never says anything or who never laughs and enjoys life. Instead, someone with the unfading loveliness of a gentle and quiet spirit speaks appropriately and wisely. She enjoys life because she is secure and at rest in her spirit. She is gracious, content, and free to give to others.

Defining a Gentle and Quiet Spirit

1. To begin developing an understanding of a gentle and quiet spirit, define the following words (use a dictionary to help you do it accurately):

   gentle—

   quiet—

   meek—(The Greek word *prays* [meek] and *praytes* [meekness] are words that consistently convey gentleness, humility, and consideration for others)[1]

   calm—

   spirit—

From your study of these words, write your own definition of a gentle and quiet spirit.

---

2. In 1 Timothy 6:11, Paul mentions gentleness as a quality to be pursued. Why do you think gentleness is included in this list?

---

3. Read 1 Thessalonians 2:5-9. How does Paul characterize his gentleness in these verses?

4. How does each of the following passages present the quality of quietness?

    Psalm 131

    Proverbs 17:1

    Isaiah 30:15

Acquiring a Gentle and Quiet Spirit

5. Read Matthew 11:28-30. What does Jesus promise us in this passage?

    What does Christ mean when He asks us to . . .

    "Come"?

    "Take My yoke"?

"Learn from Me"?

A quiet time is a time set aside to deepen your knowledge of the Lord, to enrich your own personal relationship with Him, to fellowship with Him, to love Him, to
worship Him, on a very personal basis. . . . How much of
a calm and gentle spirit you achieve, then, will depend
on how regularly and consistently, persistently and obe-
diently you partake of the Word of God, your spiritual
food.[2]

Shirley Rice

---

6. How can the following verses about God's care for us help us in acquiring
a gentle and quiet spirit?

Psalm 18:30-35

Romans 8:28

1 Corinthians 10:13

Our Lord could die with the same calm in which He had
lived. He had known all along how things would turn
out. He knew His apparent defeat would eventuate in
universal glory for the human race.

A. W. Tozer

---

7. Being secure in God's loving sovereignty is important for having a
   gentle and quiet spirit. Read Ruth 1–2:13.

   What in Ruth's life demonstrated that she was placing herself in God's
   care?

   How did God guide and protect her?

   How did Boaz describe Ruth in Ruth 3:11?

Rest is not a hallowed feeling that comes over us in
church; it is the repose of a heart set deep in God.[3]

Henry Drummond

Keeping a Gentle and Quiet Spirit

8. Below is a list of hindrances that keep me from being calm and gentle. You may want to add to the list. Look up the Scriptures and write out key thoughts from each passage in your own words. Then use this part of the study to check yourself when you sense your spirit becoming restless and irritated.

   a. Unconfessed sin — Psalm 32:3-5

   b. Anger — Ephesians 4:26

   c. An unforgiving spirit — Ephesians 4:32

   d. Self-centeredness — Philippians 2:3-4

   e. Anxiety — Philippians 4:6-7

There is a perfect passivity which is not indolence. It is a living stillness born of trust. Quiet tension is not trust. It is simply compressed anxiety.[4]

Mrs. Charles E. Cowman

f. Neglecting responsibilities—Proverbs 31:27

g. Fatigue—Psalm 127:1-2

h. Physical disorders—2 Corinthians 12:7-10

AUTHOR'S REFLECTION—I visited the beautiful home of a friend one day and that afternoon I was irritable. As I examined my heart to try to find the cause of my frustration, I realized that I was envious, jealous, and discontent with my own home. All of these responses are real enemies of a gentle and quiet spirit!

I find anxiety creeping up on me when I get in a hurry or I have over-committed myself and I cannot get everything done. When I neglect to do the wash, clean the house, or write letters as I should, then I start to become frustrated. When I stay up late and don't get enough rest, it is very hard for me to be kind and gentle. When I become harsh and critical, I ask the Lord to show me why I'm that way. Most of the time the source of my irritability is one of the hindrances mentioned above. Sometimes He has gently reminded me that I have not been spending enough time with Him and His Word, for it is in abiding in Christ that the Holy Spirit is able to produce gentleness in my life. I think that Proverbs 31:25 is a good summation of a gentle and quiet spirit: "Strength and dignity are her clothing, and she smiles at the future."

9. Look back over this chapter and write your thoughts concerning your goal of acquiring and keeping a gentle and quiet spirit. Include specific ways that you can begin to incorporate into your life that equanimity of spirit which is so precious to God.

SUGGESTED SCRIPTURE MEMORY: 1 Peter 3:3-4

I have noticed that wherever there has been a faithful following of the Lord in a consecrated soul, several things have, sooner or later, inevitably followed. Meekness and quietness of spirit become in time the characteristics of the daily life. A submissive acceptance of the will of God, as it comes in the hourly events of each day, is manifested; pliability in the hands of God to do or to suffer all the good pleasure of His will; sweetness under provocation; calmness in the midst of turmoil and bustle; a yielding to the wishes of others, and an insensibility to slights and affronts; absence of worry or anxiety; deliverance from care and fear, —all these, and many other similar graces, are invariably found to be the natural outward development of that inward life which is hid with Christ in God.[5]

Hannah Whitall Smith

Notes

1. William Klein, "Greek Word Study," in *The Small Group Letter,* Vol. 1, No. 2, May 1984, 6.

2. Shirley Rice, *The Christian Home: A Woman's View* (Norfolk, Va: Norfolk Christian Schools, 1965).

3. Henry Drummond, in *Streams in the Desert,* 176.

4. Mrs. Charles E. Cowman, *Streams in the Desert,* 108.

5. Hannah Whitall Smith, *The Christian's Secret of a Happy Life,* 201.

excellence

PERFECTED BY PURITY

Watch over your heart with all diligence, for from it flow the springs of life.
PROVERBS 4:23

To know, experience, or see God has been the deep desire and long-ing of all who truly love God. Paul wrote, "I count all things to be loss in view of the surpassing value of knowing Christ Jesus my Lord" (Philippians 3:8). In the Sermon on the Mount Jesus taught that those who are pure in heart will see God. To be holy is to be morally blameless, to be separated from sin and therefore consecrated to God. "God has provided all we need for our pursuit of holiness," writes Jerry Bridges. "He has delivered us from the reign of sin and given us His indwelling Holy Spirit. He has revealed His will for holy living in His Word, and He works in us to will and to act according to His good purpose."[1] The challenge today is being pure in such a crooked and perverse generation! What help and encouragement can we receive from the Scriptures in our goal of perfecting excellence through purity?

God's Desire for Purity

1. What attribute of God is emphasized in the following verses?

    Psalm 99:3,5,9

    Isaiah 6:3

    Isaiah 57:15

    Hebrews 7:26

---

2. Ephesians 5:1 states, "Therefore be imitators of God, as beloved children." God desires that we bear an increasing resemblance to Himself. From each of the following passages, select one truth that seems most significant to you related to becoming "imitators" of God's holiness and purity.

    Ephesians 5:3-4

    1 Thessalonians 4:3-8

Hebrews 12:14

1 Peter 1:13-16

By faith and obedience, by constant meditation on the holiness of God, by loving righteousness and hating iniquity, by a growing acquaintance with the Spirit of holiness, we can acclimate ourselves to the fellowship of the saints on earth and prepare ourselves for the eternal companionship of God and the saints above.[2]

A. W. Tozer

God's Design for Purity

3. What are the major battlefields or stumbling blocks we face in our goal of purity?

Mark 7:15,20-23

Ephesians 6:12

James 1:13-16

1 John 2:15-16

On which battlefield do you most often find yourself?

---

4. What do the following verses teach us about rejecting sin?

Romans 6:11-14

Colossians 3:1-5

1 John 3:7-9

Elisabeth Elliot writes concerning the characteristics of the old nature listed in Colossians 3:5, "These are the products of human desire, if human desire is given free reign. The Christian has handed the reins over to his Master. His human desires are brought into line. The desires still exist, are still strong, natural and human, but they are subjugated to the higher power of the Spirit. They are purified and corrected as we live day by day in faith and obedience."[3]

5. In dealing with temptation, we are often told to make a specific response to God and also respond in a specific way to Satan or our old nature. Look up the following verses and write the proper response in the appropriate column.

Verse	Response to God	Response to old self or Satan
Ephesians 6:10-11	Put on the full armor of God	Stand firm against the Devil's schemes
Colossians 3:9-10		
James 4:7		
1 Peter 5:8-9		

To experience joy, we must make some choices. We must choose to forsake sin, not only because it is defeating to us, but because it grieves the heart of God. We must choose to count on the fact that we are dead to sin, freed from its reign and dominion, and we can now actually say no to sin. We must choose to accept our responsibility to discipline our lives for obedience.[4]

Jerry Bridges

AUTHOR'S REFLECTION—Several years ago there was a television mini-series entitled *East of Eden*. As I read the promotional advertisements, I felt a desire to view this program. The line of my thinking was this: "It's based on the Bible, it would be interesting to see how the writers portray the conflict of Cain and Abel, so you should watch the series and critique it." As I read, though, I realized that there were seduction scenes and parts of the movie that were probably not honoring to God. I did not see *East of Eden* and I may have been too quick to judge, but as I prayed, I knew in my heart that it was not right for me.

I want to share a definition of sin from Susanna Wesley that has guided me and helped me immensely, especially in the "gray" areas:

"*Sin*—Whatever weakens your reason, impairs the tenderness of your conscience, obscures your sense of God, or takes off the relish of spiritual things, that thing is sin for you, however innocent it may be in itself."

It's not that all novels, television, and music are evil. Paul wrote in 1 Corinthians 6:12: "As a Christian I may do anything, but that does not mean that everything is good for me. I may do everything, but I must not be a slave of anything" (PH). The question for the committed Christian is, How will this book or program influence my walk with God and my thought life?

Another aspect of purity that I have to constantly evaluate is the subtlety of compromise and comparison. Often I think, "Well, at least I don't do that," or "I'm not as bad as many others," or "My little sins are nothing compared to what *she* does!" The thought that helps me is that I should look at my own purity not by comparing it to others', but to Christ's. Jesus said, "For I always do what pleases him" (John 8:29, NIV). Andrew Bonar wrote: "It is not the importance of the thing, but the majesty of the Lawgiver, that is to be the standard of obedience. . . . Is He a holy Lawgiver?"

The challenge and question is found in Scripture: "Who can find a virtuous woman? For her price is far above rubies" (Proverbs 31:10, KJV).

---

6. The importance of the mind in relation to purity is emphasized in the following verses. What specific instruction is given?

Psalm 119:9-11

Philippians 4:8

Our sense of sin is in proportion to our nearness to
God.

Thomas Bernard

---

7. It is important to be fully aware of the sin around us. In your own
words, write down what these verses encourage us to do that will help
us in this area.

Proverbs 4:23

Ephesians 6:13

1 Peter 5:8-9

One of the ways that I have learned to guard my heart, to be fully armored,
and to be on the alert is to consistently abide in Christ and His Word.

If there is an Enemy of Souls (and I have not the slight-
est doubt that there is), one thing he cannot abide is the
desire for purity. Hence a man's or a woman's passions
become his battleground. The Lover of Souls does not
prevent this. I was perplexed because it seemed to me He
should prevent it, but He doesn't. He wants us to learn
to use our weapons.[5]

Elisabeth Elliot

---

8. Many years ago I realized that I must have convictions concerning
   different areas of purity in my life. Pray about, think over, and write
   down your convictions in regard to:

   • your relationships with men:

   • your dress:

   • your speech:

   • your activities:

9. Proverbs 16:2 in the *New Living Translation* states, "People may be pure in their own eyes, but the LORD examines their motives."

   a. What does this verse tell us about 1) what *should* and 2) what *should not* be the source of our standard of purity?

   b. In what personal areas do you find yourself most susceptible to setting your own standards of thought or conduct without seeking God's guidance?

   Asking yourself the following questions may be helpful in discerning your motives and choosing that which is pure.

   • Is it helpful—physically, spiritually, and mentally? (1 Corinthians 6:12)

   • Does it bring me under its power? (1 Corinthians 6:12)

   • Does it hurt others? (1 Corinthians 8:13)

   • Does it glorify God? (1 Corinthians 10:31)

   • Can I do it in His name? (Colossians 3:17)

God's Delight in Purity

10. According to the following verses, what are the results of living a pure life?

Psalm 24:3-5

Matthew 5:8

> It is quite true to say—"I cannot live a holy life," but you can decide to let Jesus Christ make you holy.[6]
>
> *Oswald Chambers*

Thoughts for Spiritual Encouragement

Some precious words of an old hymn tell us that God's grace is greater than all our sin. Perhaps there has been some impurity in your past. The Scriptures state, "If we confess our sins, He is faithful and righteous to forgive us our sins and to cleanse us from all unrighteousness" (1 John 1:9). Our confession brings cleansing.

To encourage our own purity it is wise to have friends who practice purity. To help in areas of vulnerability it is good to have someone you can call or go to for special prayer.

11. Perhaps you would like to write out a prayer to God expressing your desire to live a holy life. You might want to include some thoughts from the old hymn that follows.

More purity give me, More strength to o'er-come;
More freedom from earth stains,
More longings for home;
More fit for the kingdom, More used would I be;
More blessed and holy; More, Savior, like Thee.

P. P. Bliss

SUGGESTED SCRIPTURE MEMORY: Proverbs 4:23

Notes

1. Jerry Bridges, *The Pursuit of Holiness* (Colorado Springs: NavPress, 1984), 157.

2. A. W. Tozer, *The Knowledge of the Holy.*

3. Elisabeth Elliot, *Passion and Purity* (Old Tappan, N.J.: Fleming H. Revell, 1984), 94.

4. Bridges, 157.

5. Elliot, 26.

6. Oswald Chambers, *My Utmost for His Highest,* July 9.

excellence

Proclaimed by Wisdom

But the wisdom from above is first pure, then peaceable, gentle, reasonable, full of mercy and good fruits, unwavering, without hypocrisy.

JAMES 3:17

James gives us a beautiful description of wisdom in James 3:17. His definition could be a good summation of our study of excellence. Wisdom, as we will be studying, "depends on right conduct in obedience to the will of God rather than theoretical insight."[1] The word "wise" in Greek comes from *sophos*, which describes "one with moral insight and skill in the practical issues of life."[2] Larry Crabb defines wisdom as "belief that accepting God's way, no matter how painful, leads ultimately to joy." He defines foolishness as refusing to believe that "going our way, even though it genuinely relieves distress and feels good, leads ultimately to despair."[3] The dictionary tells us that wisdom is "the power of judging rightly and following the soundest course of action based on knowledge, experience, and understanding." Certainly wisdom in our lives will be the proclamation of excellence.

Essentials of Wisdom

1. According to the following passages, what is the foundational requirement for acquiring wisdom?

   Proverbs 9:10

   Proverbs 15:33

   Job 28:28

> Fearing the Lord means having a deep reverence and respect for God and His Word, a respect and reverence that result in obedience.[4]
>
> *Bill Hammer*

2. a. Who is wisdom? (Consult the following verses.)

   1 Corinthians 1:30

   Colossians 2:2-3

b. What would be a necessary conclusion from these verses for our becoming wise?

---

3. Read James 3:13-18.

a. In the appropriate columns, note the various aspects of the wisdom of the world and the wisdom from above. (You might find it helpful to read several translations.)

Wisdom of the World	Wisdom from Above

b. How is wisdom to be shown in our lives (verse 13)?

Lord,
Open my ears!
So much of what I read in your Word speaks
of the importance of hearing.
Wisdom demands it;
Righteousness requires it;
Understanding necessitates it.
I see so much of selective hearing.
Am I a selective listener?
Do I only hear what I want to?
Oh, Father!
You know I long to be
wise,
understanding,
discerning.
Teach me to hear from people,
experiences,
expressions,
tones from life . . .
With an openness of mind,
a totality of heart,
and an abandonment of my own preconceived ideas.
Help me to learn.
Teach me to open my ears and really hear.[5]

Carole Mayhall

Acquiring Wisdom

4. What can you do to begin to grow in wisdom?

Proverbs 2:1-10

Proverbs 3:5-6

Proverbs 13:20

Proverbs 22:17

Matthew 7:24-25

Colossians 3:16

James 1:5-6

With the goodness of God to desire our highest welfare, the wisdom of God to plan it, what do we lack? Surely we are the most favored of all creatures.[6]

A. W. Tozer

5. As you consider your answers to question 4, what are your strengths in acquiring wisdom?

Your weaknesses?

What can you do to improve your growth in wisdom?

Characteristics of Wisdom

6. James 3:13 states, "Who among you is wise and understanding? Let him show by his good behavior his deeds in the gentleness of wisdom." Use the following chart to help you understand how your behavior can reflect God's wisdom. In the first column, briefly write out what the verse says. Then, summarize in the second column what the general principle is by stating in your own words what your need is in this area. Finally, fill in the third column with a possible application you might feel God wants you to take in order to grow in the kind of behavior that shows wisdom and understanding.

Verse(s)	Behavioral Characteristics	My Need	Possible Application
Proverbs 29:11	Keeps himself under control	Not to let my emotions control my behavior	Ask God to help me respond in a godly way to pressure, without emotional outbursts/Memorize Proverbs 29:11
Psalm 90:12 Ephesians 5:15-17			
Proverbs 12:18 10:31 10:19			
Proverbs 9:9 10:8 12:15			
Proverbs 9:8 15:31			
Proverbs 11:30			

AUTHOR'S REFLECTION—In Proverbs 2 we are told that if we seek and search for wisdom then we will discover the knowledge of God, for the Lord gives wisdom to the upright. Seeking, searching, and asking for wisdom are keys to our becoming wise. Oswald Chambers observes, "We will never receive if we ask with an end in view; if we ask, not out of our poverty but out of our lust."[7] Our desire to be wise must spring from a heart whose sole purpose is to know our awesome God and to please Him, not self. For I believe that as we truly seek this wisdom from above, then all the characteristics of wisdom will begin to be manifested in our lives. The emphasis must be on our diligent search, our commitment to all that wisdom is, and our realization that growing in wisdom is a lifelong process.

> To break with all worldly customs; to live utterly separate from the spirit of the world, so that we shall not say, "What is the harm of this and that?" but simply shall have lost all relish for what is not of the Father; to live as those who truly lay all on the altar—time, strength, possessions, literally everything we are and have; to live, not nominally but truly, in unity; this will cost us something. Are we ready for what it will cost?[8]
>
> *Amy Carmichael*

Benefits of Wisdom

7. Wisdom is not without its benefits. Read the following verses and list the fruits of wisdom.

   Proverbs 3:13-18

Proverbs 8:12,17-21

Proverbs 8:32-35

When looking back on the lives of men and women of God the tendency is to say—What wonderfully astute wisdom they had! How perfectly they understood all God wanted! The astute mind behind is the Mind of God, not human wisdom at all. We give credit to human wisdom when we should give credit to the Divine guidance of God through childlike people who were foolish enough to trust God's wisdom and the supernatural equipment of God.[9]

Oswald Chambers

SUGGESTED SCRIPTURE MEMORY: James 3:17

Notes

1. *The New International Dictionary of New Testament Theology*, Vol. 3, 1028.

2. *The Bible Knowledge Commentary*.

3. Larry Crabb, in a seminar at Glen Eyrie, Colorado Springs, January 1984.

4. Bill Hammer, "Take a Drink from the Fountain of Wisdom," *Discipleship Journal*, Vol. 2, No. 5, September 1982, 8.

5. Carole Mayhall, *Lord, Teach Me Wisdom* (Colorado Springs: NavPress, 1979), 48-49.

6. A. W. Tozer, *The Knowledge of the Holy*, 70.

7. Oswald Chambers, *My Utmost for His Highest*, June 9.

8. Amy Carmichael, *Thou Givest . . . They Gather*, 199.

9. Chambers, 300.

PART FOUR

THE

PRAISE

excellence

PORTRAYED IN THE LIFE OF A GODLY WOMAN

Many daughters have done nobly, but you excel them all.

PROVERBS 31:29

I hope that as you have studied *Becoming a Woman of Excellence*, you have sensed that our lives are precious to God, so precious that He has given us specific guidelines to keep our hearts pure and open before Him. In a beautiful "last act" in His book on wisdom, God draws a portrait of a woman who epitomizes excellence. The Proverbs 31 woman exemplifies one who was disciplined, discreet, wise, strong, and gracious. Above all she feared God; she revered Him with her life.

Speaking of the woman in Proverbs 31, Derek Kidner wrote, "Her charm and her success owe nothing to chance, because her outlook and her influence have the solid foundation of the fear and wisdom of God."[1] Truly this woman is an example of one whose goal was to fear God and pursue excellence.

A Pattern of Excellence

1. Read Proverbs 31:10-31. In the space provided next to the corresponding verses, write down a suggested character quality that motivated the Proverbs 31 woman to do what she did. (The Proverbs 31 woman was married, but the spiritual qualities of her life speak to all women, whether married or single. If you are single, in place of husband and children in these verses, you can substitute family or friends. Whose heart is trusting in you? Who are you committed to in order to serve and minister to as the Proverbs 31 woman did to her family?)

   verses 11-15

   verses 16-20

   verses 21-24

   verses 25-27

   verses 28-31

AUTHOR'S REFLECTION—As I have studied and meditated on Proverbs 31, I think that I discovered one of the secrets of this woman's excellence—she realized that she could really only control her life. Her responses, her walk with God, were her responsibility and not dependent on anyone else. Larry Crabb has defined a *goal*—something I want that I can control and a *desire*—something I want that I cannot control.[2]

If I want to lose weight, that is a legitimate goal because I am solely responsible for what I eat and whether I exercise. If I want a friend or loved one to lose weight, that can only be a desire because I cannot control his or her eating or exercising! There is nothing wrong with desires, but it is very important to discern the difference between goals and desires in our life. A goal is something that I can be totally responsible for; I do not have to depend on anyone else to get that goal accomplished. (In a friendship or marriage, I cannot have a goal of having a good friendship/ marriage because that involves someone else—it can be a desire, however, and as such I can pray and cooperate in the relationship to make it so. A proper goal for me in a friendship is to be a good friend and in marriage to be a good wife because that is something I can control.)

We begin to have problems when we confuse our desires and goals. Whenever we try to make a desire a goal and someone blocks it, we get angry and frustrated—mainly because we aren't getting our own way!

I think that Proverbs 31 is a model for taking responsibility for our part in living a godly life. The chapter is full of "she does, she seeks, she is, she brings, she stretches." It is good to examine our responses in different situations to see if we are trying to control or manipulate someone else. Richard Foster has written, "We must come to the place in our lives where we lay down the everlasting burden of needing to manage others." My being an excellent woman does not really depend on anyone else: it depends on my deciding that I will be God's woman who fears Him, who derives her worth and security from Christ, and who is then free to serve and love others.

2. Considering this woman's life and our previous study, what do you think is most essential to becoming a woman of excellence?

The priority in this woman's life is seen in verse 30 — her fear of God. It is her spiritual life that is commended and is foundational to her excellence. She and Mary of Bethany in Luke 10 chose the "good portion," and so must we.

A Pursuit of Excellence

The suggested Scripture memory verse for this chapter is Proverbs 31:30. However, now that you have finished this study, I would like to encourage you to take a block of time and memorize Proverbs 31:10-31. It has been a blessing to me, and the Lord has used many verses to encourage me at special times.

3. In the first chapter of our study, you were asked to write a personal goal for this study. This may be a good time to review your goal. After studying many aspects of excellence and now understanding the difference between a goal and a desire, perhaps you would like to write a goal for your life. When you have prayerfully considered this goal, you may want to write it in the front of your Bible, so that you can be reminded of your commitment to God.

    My Goal:

AUTHOR'S REFLECTION—I would like to share the goal I have set for my life: "My goal is to honor the Lord in my thoughts, speech, actions, and activities, to exemplify Christ's character as I respond to people and circumstances, and to continually deepen my fellowship and knowledge of God and His Word."

Betty Scott Stam and her husband John were missionaries to China in the early 1940s. When the Communist Red Guard took over China, they beheaded both Betty and her husband. Following is Betty's life goal, which has challenged many to pursue excellence:

"Lord, I give up all my own plans and purposes, all my own desires and hopes, and accept Thy will for my life. I give myself, my life, my all utterly to Thee to be Thine forever. Fill me and seal me with Thy Holy Spirit. Use me as Thou wilt, send me where Thou wilt, work out Thy whole will in my life at any cost, now and forever."

> My goal is God Himself, not joy nor peace, nor even blessing, but Himself, my God.[3]
>
> *Oswald Chambers*

Notes

1. Derek Kidner, *Proverbs: An Introduction and Commentary,* Tyndale Old Testament Commentaries (Downers Grove: InterVarsity, 1979), 184.

2. Larry Crabb, in a seminar at Glen Eyrie, Colorado Springs, January 1984.

3. Oswald Chambers, *My Utmost for His Highest,* November 17.

Is Thine Heart Set on Ascents?

His thoughts said, The rocks are far too steep for me. I cannot climb.

His Father said, "With Me as thy Guide, thou canst. I have not given thee the spirit of fear, but of power and of love and of discipline. Whence then this spirit of fear?"

His thoughts said, But who shall ascend into the hill of the Lord, or who shall rise up in His holy Place? Shall I ever pass the foothills?

His Father said, "Is thine heart set on ascents?"

The son answered, "O Lord, Thou knowest."

And the Father comforted him, "Commit thy way—thy way to the summit—to thy Lord. Only let thine heart be set on ascents."

And the Father added, "Dear son, I will keep thine heart set on ascents."

Amy Carmichael

A GUIDE FOR
BIBLE STUDY LEADERS

*A*s you lead your group, keep in mind the purpose of this study: to motivate a pursuit of excellence in our Christian pilgrimage, to realize that this pursuit is a lifelong process, and to learn to make specific applications of the Scriptures to our lives. A wholehearted and serious approach to applying what is learned should produce growth and change. Hopefully, when you finish the study your group will not be the same as when you began! Your group purpose should be to provide insights, challenges, accountability, and prayer support for one another.

Within each chapter are subheadings, which can serve as discussion topics. You might begin each session by asking the group's key thoughts, new insights, or questions concerning the topics raised by these subheadings. As you do your own study before each meeting, you might also want to prepare specific questions for each section. Commentaries and a Bible dictionary can be resources for added information and clarification. Of course your greatest resource is sensitivity to the Holy Spirit as He guides and directs the study according to the needs of the group.

Here is a suggested outline for your first meeting:

1. Have each member introduce herself and tell about her family and her Christian experience.

2. Pass out the books and look at the format of the study. Note the table of contents, quotations from Christian writers and thinkers, author's reflections, Scripture memory, and personal applications in each chapter.

3. Explain that the Scripture memory verse for each lesson is printed out under the chapter title. Writing the verse on a 3" x 5" card in the translation they choose can be helpful. The card can be placed over the kitchen sink or carried easily to memorize at different times during the day. In order to review the memory verse, try dividing the group into pairs to recite the Scripture at the beginning of each lesson.

4. As a group, you might want to set standards for your time together. These standards could include commitment to attendance, Scripture memory, completing each chapter, and diligence in application.

5. Ask the group's thoughts on having prayer partners during the study. These partners would not have to meet together outside of the group sessions, but they could share requests during the week. You might draw numbers to determine who would be partners.

6. Close in prayer.

AUTHOR

Cynthia Hall Heald is a native Texan. She and her husband, Jack, a veterinarian by profession, are on full-time staff with The Navigators in Tucson, Arizona. They have four children: Melinda, Daryl, Shelly, and Michael.

Cynthia graduated from the University of Texas with a BA in English. She speaks frequently to church women's groups and at seminars and retreats.

Cynthia is also the author of the NavPress Bible studies *Becoming a Woman of Freedom*, *Becoming a Woman of Purpose*, *Becoming a Woman of Prayer*, *Intimacy with God*, and *Loving Your Husband* (companion study to *Loving Your Wife* by Jack and Cynthia), and *Becoming a Woman Who Walks with God*.

ALSO BY CYNTHIA HEALD

Dwelling in His Presence (2009, NavPress)
Becoming a Woman of Simplicity (2009, NavPress)
Becoming a Woman Who Loves (2009, NavPress)
Becoming a Woman of Faith (2009, NavPress)
Becoming a Woman of Grace (2009, NavPress)
Intimacy with God (2000, NavPress)
Loving Your Husband (1989, NavPress)
Walking Together (2000, NavPress)
Loving Your Wife, with Jack Heald (1989, NavPress)
Becoming a Woman of Freedom (2005, NavPress)
Becoming a Woman of Purpose (2005, NavPress)
Becoming a Woman of Prayer (2005, NavPress)
Becoming a Woman Who Walks with God (2004, NavPress)

Eleven-week studies by Cynthia Heald!